31
Spiritual
Lessons
I Learned from
My Dog

31
Spiritual
Lessons
I Learned from
My Dog

Raylene King

Front Porch Resources
· Nolensville, Tennessee ·

ISBN 978-0-9792957-0-6

Library of Congress cataloging-in-Publication date 2007

King, Raylene

Originally published: Nolensville, Tennessee. Front Porch Resources, 2007.

ISBN 978-0-9792957-0-6 (softcover)

Library of Congress Control Number: 2007923703

To order additional copies of this resource, contact Front Porch Resources:

Mail: P.O. Box 692; Nolensville, Tennessee 37135

email: info@frontporchresources.com

Online: www.frontporchresources.com

Dedication

This book is dedicated to my husband Dennis, who always knows how to encourage me, just when to push me,and how to always be there for me. Your love makes life's joys sweeter, and the difficulties bearable. You demonstrate in human form God's unselfish love for me. I respect and admire you for so many reasons. I love you, and I truly believe that together, we can accomplish anything.

And to Cosmo, through whom I am daily learning the helplessness of the creature and the great love and compassion of the Master.

Acknowledgements

First, I would like to give praise and honor to God for showing me His timeless concepts, and for allowing me to see a picture of my own struggle with obedience or disobedience through my dealings with, of all things, a small dog. Thank You that You can use the most seemingly insignificant things to teach us about Yourself. Thank You that You have a plan for my life and that You will always direct my steps if I will just follow You.

To Dennis – thanks for all your love, support, and encouragement; thank you for all the research and leg work you did to make this book happen.

To my son Joe and Anna – thank you so much for bringing Cosmo into our lives. He has captured our hearts and taught us much. Thanks for all your support.

To my son Stephen – thank you for all your support and for encouraging us to move forward toward our dreams.

To my Mom – thank you for all the love and support you have given me for all of my life, no matter what I was endeavoring to do.

To Mom and Dad King – thank you for always being there for us. Your support means so much.

To Toni Crosby – thank you for being such a prayer warrior in my life, and for giving me the concept of this project as a 31 Day devotional book. Thank you for pushing me to finish it and guiding us through the publication process, and for sharing your editing skills with us. I treasure your friendship.

To Mike and Martha Mitchell – thanks for all your help with the set-up and formatting of this manuscript…thank you for giving of your time and talents to help make this happen.

To John and Marilynn Duran – thanks for the laptop, your encouraging words and Marilynn's invaluable help in the proofing and editing process. Your wisdom was much appreciated.

To Karen Wooten – thanks for lending proofing and editing skills to this project. I really appreciate your help.

To Cassie and Armando Vera – thanks for your amazing artwork, the sketch of Cosmo which so perfectly captures his personality, the beautiful cover design, and especially all your encouragement.

To Everyone at Stonebrook Baptist Church and especially the Wednesday Night Prayer Group: Lori, Mom, Rosemary, Dennis, Angie, Betty, Toni, Merle, Littlejohn…for all the prayers offered up for this project. Thank you for listening to my excerpts and giving me input.

To the Alumbaugh family – Tony, Cindy, Richie, and Kenner. Thank you for being Cosmo's second family and taking such great care of him.

To Beth Clark – who has an extraordinary talent for training dogs. Thank you for all your advice and efforts with our stubborn little guy!

To Dr. Gregg Harris and everyone at Chapel Hill Veterinary Services – thank you for always giving Cosmo such great care.

I'd like to thank some teachers I remember for their ability to inspire their students to do their best and for making learning fun, and also for encouraging me in my writing: Mrs. Edith Kirby, Mrs. Cathy Kemp, and Mrs. Wilma McDonald.

To Pastor Ron and Marilyn Lentine – thank you for your friendship and encouraging me to pursue my writing.

To LeAnn Bauer – for giving loving care to Cosmo.

Cosmo

Introduction

It's not that my husband and I had anything against dogs really, our lifestyle just did not seem to support having a dog. Like most people our days, and even our evenings seem to be come more jam-packed each week.

I don't know if you are aware of this fact, but dogs are a lot of work: the walking in all kinds of weather, the training, the grooming, plus the fact that everything has to be on a fairly tight schedule with little room for error. Seeing to all these needs can be very time consuming; it is a never-ending, daily routine of love and effort.

I guess we were rather spoiled after having a cat for the last several years. Now granted, cats are moody and dogs are always ready with affection. But cats are also very low maintenance. Just give them some food, water, litter box, and they'll let you know loudly if they want anything else!

Along with all the work, also to be considered is the famous negative puppy behavior; chewing, barking, and accidents everywhere!

So, like I said, nothing personal against dogs, but we just didn't think it was right for us.

That is, until our son's girlfriend Anna requested a miniature dachshund puppy for her birthday. Joe so sweetly complied, drove a couple of hours, and paid a couple hundred dollars to purchase this special gift. We were doing o.k., firm in our resolve that "We really are more cat people" until we saw that little guy who was the color of a piece of melted chocolate, and who doesn't love chocolate? Once our eyes met those brown eyes pleading "love me," we were done for.

Since Anna was in college and needed quiet to study, and since dachshunds are famous for barking, the little guy named Cosmo began to "visit" us on weekends. Eventually, because of changes in both Anna and our son Joe's living arrangements, neither of them could keep Cosmo, so they began to talk about options for him. They were discussing sending him to Chicago to live with her brother, when we realized we were totally smitten and could not stand to see him shipped up North! Besides, he's a shivery little dog and he would freeze in the Windy City!

So, we began our new occupation as full-time caretakers to this little guy. It was during some of the daily chores I mentioned earlier that I began to see some spiritual parallels developing between our dealings with Cosmo and our Master's dealings with us. I hope you can see yourself in these as well.

Lesson One

The Best Place To Be Is In The Master's Presence

The time Cosmo is absolutely the happiest is when he is either lying at our feet chewing his favorite toy,(and hopefully not our shoes), or being held in our laps while he sleeps. He wants to be constantly in our presence, even following us from room to room. He just wants to be near us; to receive our love and approval.

Can you imagine the intimacy and closeness we would have with God if we made spending time with Him our greatest desire?

Psalm 16:8a says, "I have set the Lord continually before me…" This sounds like someone who is totally committed to staying in the Lord's presence, not just dropping by for a visit occasionally.

Psalm 42:1 compares our desire for God's presence to a thirst for a drink of water,

As the deer pants for streams of water, so my soul pants for you O God–My soul thirsts for God for the living God. When can I go and meet with God?

Psalm 63:1 continues this theme of thirst,

O God, Thou art my God; I shall seek Thee earnestly, my soul thirsts for Thee, my flesh yearns for Thee.

Imagine in the heat of the day, mid-summer, after a morning of yard work, all you can think about is how good a cold glass of water would be; it becomes all you can think about, the driving force that propels you to go finish the job and get that cool, refreshing drink.

Psalm 130: 6 uses another illustration of seeking the Lord,

My soul waits for the Lord more than the watchman for the morning, indeed more than the watchman for the morning.

3

Now this verse is so easy to relate to; how many of us can recall a night when all we could do was watch for the morning? I can remember times when my son became sick during the night. The only thought that consumed me was seeing the first light of morning so we could get to the doctor's office and get some relief for him. Maybe you recall a night of trouble when there was nothing you could do but wait for morning to see how things were going to play out.

Can you see from these scriptures the intensity we must have about being in our Master's presence? We have His great and mighty promises that if we will seek Him, He will let us find Him.

Lord, please awaken within me an unquenchable thirst for Your presence. Help me to seek You and find You when I search for You with all my heart. Help me to make the choices and changes necessary in my life to enable me to have the time and focus to put You first.

"Paws"
for
Reflection

Lesson Two

The Best Way To Begin And End Your Day Is With Your Head In The Master's Lap

My husband Dennis is a bi-vocational pastor, which means he works other jobs in addition to his pastoral duties. He is currently a school bus driver for the county we live in, so he gets up very early. One of Cosmo's favorite things is to lie on his lap while he drinks his coffee before daybreak. Another cherished time is at night stretching that long body across my lap while I'm working on the computer; then some cuddles before he goes into his crate for the night.

Scripture is full of encouragement to spend time with God both in the morning and at night. Jesus Himself was an example of this for us:

Matthew 14:23
After He had dismissed them (the crowd), He went up on a mountainside by Himself to pray. When evening came, He was there alone…

Psalm 5:3
In the morning, O Lord, you hear my voice; in the morning I lay my requests before you and wait with expectation.

Psalm 55:17
Evening and morning and at noon, will I pray and cry aloud: and He shall hear my voice.

What an awesome privilege to begin our day acknowledging our Master and asking his blessing and guidance for the day, and ending our day leaving all our cares with Him and enjoying the time of rest He has prepared for us

Lord, help me to gain the wonderful benefits You have for me as I take the opportunity to seek You in the morning and in the evening. Please give me wisdom in the morning as I set the course for my day; help me to trust in You and not depend on my own strength or understanding.

7

Help me when night comes and I am tempted to let circumstances of the day just past, or worries for tomorrow steal my peace. Help me lay all my cares down and rest in You.

"*Paws*"
for
Reflection

Lesson Three

Watch For The Master's Return

When we are out of his sight, Cosmo is always watching and listening for our return. In the afternoon when Dennis comes home from his bus route, he parks the bus on the parking lot next to our house. When Cosmo hears the noise of the air brake, he knows the Master has returned. He stands at the front door watching expectantly and listening for the key to turn in the door. His joy is boundless as he waits for the reward he knows is coming when he sees Dennis, the long-awaited fellowship he longs for. The Bible has many reminders for us about watching and waiting for our Master's return:

Matthew 24:42 says,

Therefore keep watch, because you do not know on what day your Lord will come.

Matthew 25:13 echoes this thought,

Therefore keep watch, because you do not know the day or the hour.

Just like Cosmo can sense the time of day approaching when Dennis will return, and just like the sound of the motor turning off and the air brake signal his arrival, Jesus told us the signs we should look for preceding His return so we would not be caught off guard. We are to be always watchful and ready.

Lord, give me wisdom to discern the signs that Your coming is near. Give me listening ears, watchful eyes, and a longing heart for Your return. Fill my heart with peace even though circumstances in the world are far from peaceful. Help me remember that You have promised to come back for me, and that You never fail to keep even one of Your promises.

"Paws"
for
Reflection

Lesson Four

Be Content With What You Have

It really doesn't take a lot of stuff to make Cosmo happy. He just needs a few well-chewed toys, food, water, a soft bed, and our love and affection. Similarly, we will be happier if we keep our wants and needs simple.

More is not necessarily better, in fact sometimes "more" or the quest for it causes a lot of stress in our lives. We become obsessed with getting more, bigger, and better; consequently, our peace of mind, family relationships, finances, health, and our spiritual well being all suffer in the process. God's Word is able to guide us along the path to balance in this area:

Philippians 4:11-12 tells us,

I am not saying this because I am in need, for I have learned to be content whatever the circumstances; For I know what it is to be in need, and I know what it is to have plenty. I have learned the secret of being content in any and every situation whether well fed or hungry, whether living in plenty or in want.

I Timothy 6:6 adds,

But godliness with contentment is great gain.

2 Timothy 6:8
But if we have food and clothing, we will be content with that.

Hebrews 13:5 admonishes us,

Keep your lives free from the love of money and be content with what you have, because God has said, "Never will I leave you."

Lord, help me not to define myself by, or let my happiness be based on, the amount of things that I have. Show me how to be content with what I have, and not be focused on things I don't have or really even need. Help me to realize that the things that really matter are the gifts You have given me of friends, family, and the most priceless gift of eternal life through Your Son, Jesus. Thank You.

"Paws"
for
Reflection

Lesson Five

There Is No Need To Worry

We have had our dog for a year and a half now, and I have never seen him pacing around worrying if we are going to give him what he needs. He simply trusts us, his master, to take care of his needs. We have proven to him that we are worthy of his trust by consistently, day after day, meeting his basic needs. How much more has our heavenly Master proven Himself trustworthy in caring for His children all throughout history and to this very day. In Matthew 6:25-34 we see a beautiful picture of the provider who cares for the birds of the air and even the flowers of the field and who also cares for our needs:

Therefore I tell you, do not worry about your life, what you will eat or drink; or about your body, what you will wear. Is not life more important than food, and the body more important than clothes? Look at the birds of the air; they do not sow or reap or store away in barns and yet your heavenly Father feeds them. Are you not much more valuable than they?

Who of you can by worrying add a single hour to his life? And why do you worry about clothes? See how the lilies of the field grow. They do not labor or spin. Yet I tell you that not even Solomon in all his splendor was dressed like one of them. If that is how God clothes the grass of the field which is here today and tomorrow is thrown into the fire, will He not much more clothe you, O you of little faith? So do not worry saying, "What shall we eat?" or "What shall we drink?" or "What shall we wear?" For the pagans run after all these things, and your heavenly Father knows that you need them. But seek first His kingdom and His righteousness, and all these things will be given you.

Lord, how it must grieve You when You see the way I continue to worry about the daily matters of life in spite of all Your Word has to say about Your ability and desire to meet all my needs. Please make me aware every time worry begins to creep into my thinking. Help me to stop it then and there, and to rest in Your promise of provision and peace.

"Paws"
for
Reflection

Lesson Six

The Master Knows Your Needs and What Is Best For You

Can you imagine our dog Cosmo saying to us, "Can we talk? I have some questions and concerns about your recent choices for me. You've changed dog food brands, changed the route of my walk, you haven't given me a new toy in ages. How can I be sure you have my best interest at heart?"

How ludicrous that the creature would dare to question the wisdom or motives of the Master, right? Do you see anything the slightest bit familiar about the previous dialogue? How often do we express our displeasure to God either consciously or perhaps unconsciously by our attitudes and actions?

Thanks to God, He is always full of loving-kindness and mercy toward us. He listens to our complaints just as a loving parent listens to a whining child or even one having a full-blown tantrum . Then when we have vented our feelings and usually feel worse, not better, for having done so, He gathers us up and assures us of His incomparable love for us. A love that is so great it could never give anything but blessings to us; a love He has proven with the gift of His own Son.

What does scripture have to show us about God's motives toward us?

Matthew 7:11 says,

If you, then, though you are evil, know how to give good gifts to your children, how much more will your Father in heaven give good gifts to those who ask Him!

Philippians 4:11
And my God shall supply all your needs according to His glorious riches in Christ Jesus.

Jeremiah 29:11 leaves no question when it says,

"For I know the plans I have for you," declares the Lord, "plans to prosper you and not to harm you, plans to give you hope and a future."

17

We can truly rest in His goodness and love.

Lord, please forgive me when I foolishly question Your motives or methods in my life. Help me to understand the depth of Your knowledge of me personally: my needs, my likes, and my dislikes. You created me and know what I need each moment. I know that I can trust You because Your greatest desire is to always do me good and never evil.

You will never withhold any good thing that fits in with Your plan for my life.

"Paws"
for
Reflection

Lesson Seven

Seek And Give
Forgiveness Quickly

Dogs are so quick to forgive, and in their own way, to ask for forgiveness. You know that drooping tail, lowered head, and sad eyes that come along with your chewed up shoe? They care if you are angry; they want the loving, normal relationship to be restored. They don't want you to be angry with them. They want things back like they were before the offense occurred.

Dogs are also very quick to forgive when they have been offended, whether it was an accidental step on the tail, or perhaps sharp words hurled after some disobedience. They aren't really content until everything is right again. Can you see how much more peace we would have in our lives on a daily basis if this was our attitude toward giving and receiving forgiveness? We too can only be truly happy when things are right between us and the people we live in contact with; and more importantly between our Master and us.

Mark 11:25 instructs us,

And when you stand praying, if you hold anything against anyone, forgive him, so that your Father in heaven may forgive your sins.

Colossians 3:13 continues this theme,

Bear with each other and forgive whatever grievances you may have against another. Forgive as the Lord forgave you.

I John 1:9 is a beautiful verse, it says,

If we confess our sins, he is faithful and just and will forgive us our sins and purify us from all unrighteousness.

Through God's assistance and power, we can forgive and seek forgiveness.

Lord, why is it that the greatest gift we can receive, forgiveness, can also be the hardest gift for us to give to others? Help me to realize that as You have freely forgiven me, I also have to extend forgiveness to others; that keeping a "clean slate" with You and with those around me is the only way I can be truly happy and free. Remind me that having an unforgiving heart is really a prison I hold myself in and that only I can turn the key by forgiving the wrongs done to me. Thank you above all that Your forgiveness is always available to me.

"Paws"
for
Reflection

Lesson Eight

Everything Belongs To The Master

A few months ago, we decided our undisciplined little "wiener dog" needed some obedience classes. We worked on various problem areas including: barking, chewing things up, coming when called, and walking obediently on our daily walks.

One very interesting concept the trainer brought to our attention was that Cosmo had to learn that we were the "leaders of the pack" and not him! This was to be accomplished through a series of leader exercises.

Now this was an entirely new concept to a very stubborn little dachshund who had all but already hung a sign on his dog house that read, "The Boss"! It was very important for him to realize that everything was ours, it all belonged to us, and he was only entitled to what we chose to give him.

If we give and receive things with an open hand, we will live happier, more peaceful lives. The key is to realize that all we have really doesn't belong to us at all. It all belongs to the Master who graciously gives to us from His hand.

In Job 34:13 we find one of Job's friends asking,

Who appointed Him over the earth? Who put Him in charge of the whole world?

Psalm 24:1 says,

The earth is the Lord's and everything in it, the world, and all who live in it; for He founded it upon the seas and established it upon the waters.

Psalm 83:18
Let them know that you, whose name is the Lord are the Most High over all the earth.

There is no good thing outside God's desire and ability to give it to us. We just need to rest in His goodness toward us and trust His timing, which is always perfect.

Lord, You are so kind and gracious to me. You share your great bounty of blessings with me. I have nothing on my own , even the very air I breathe to exist belongs to You. You are the Creator, yet you graciously open Your hand and care for me, a helpless, needy creature. How can I ever thank You for Your goodness toward me?

"Paws"
for
Reflection

_____

_____

_____

_____

_____

_____

_____

Lesson Nine

If You Get Out From Under the Master's Umbrella, You Get Cold and Wet

Rainy day walks are not one of Cosmo's favorite things. He would much prefer to stay dry and warm inside, even though I have this huge, blue umbrella to give us shelter as we walk.

We start our off on our walk with things going pretty well, walking in sync, both under the umbrella I am holding. However, before long, Cosmo decides to head off on his own to explore some stick or favorite patch of grass. This usually leads him out from under the umbrella and into the cold, falling rain.

When I try to pull him back under the protection of the umbrella, he resists until the wetness of his fur becomes uncomfortable enough to compel him to obedience.

In the same way, God has set protective barriers around us and coverings over us. The protection can take various forms: certainly the Word of God is a major protection for us if we will know it and walk in it, also the wise advice of godly friends, the examples of others who have gone before us, and moral rules and restrictions as well as our civil laws.

Does God allow us the free choice to move out from under His protection if we choose to? Yes He does, and hopefully, just like Cosmo, when we get wet and cold enough, we will come back to the shelter of the Master's covering.

Psalm 41:2 says,
The Lord will protect him and preserve his life; he will bless him in the land and not surrender him to the desires of his foes.

Psalm 32:7
You are my hiding place; You will protect me from trouble and surround me with songs of deliverance.

Psalm 91:14
"Because he loves Me," says the LORD, "I will rescue him; I will protect him, for he acknowledges my name."

Lord, out of Your great love for me, You have set protective coverings for me. I know I sometimes stray out from under them. I am so grateful for the loving mercy You show me while I am wandering, and especially for the way You welcome me back with open arms. Thank You for not letting me be comfortable anywhere but the exact place where You are, and where You want me to be.

"Paws"
for
Reflection

_____

_____

_____

_____

_____

_____

_____

Lesson Ten

The Master Holds The Leash

I have a feeling that were it not for the leash I hold firmly in my hand on our walks, we would not have our furry, little friend for very long. Left to his own choices and impetuous actions, he would surely run into traffic or get too close to some bigger, unfriendly dog and be done in by his own flawed decision.

Fortunately, the firm pressure I hold on the leash keeps him from harm. Here is the tricky part, sometimes he complies easily to the pressure of the leash and we go quickly on our way. Sometimes he pulls away just out of innocent curiosity-he just has to get a closer sniff! And sometimes, he looks at me, sets himself for a fight and out of pure rebellion challenges me to "go ahead, make my day, make me move your way"! Do you recognize anybody here, like each of us maybe?

The Master doesn't hold tight rein on the leash to punish or prohibit us, but for our protection. When we pull on the leash and try to go our own way, we only hurt ourselves. The bottom line is, how much pain do we want to inflict on ourselves before we comply?

We can do it the easy way or the hard way. The easy way is God's way, we stop resisting and pulling in the other direction, and let Him lead us; because He loves us and He knows the destination we are heading toward. The hard way is our way, we pull on the leash, exhausting ourselves, chaffing our necks and still not getting anywhere. The response of the creature determines the amount of pull from the Master necessary to get them moving in the right direction again.

The scriptures have a lot to say about the results of either our obedience or rebellion to His leading:

Job 36:11-12 says
If they obey and serve Him, they will spend the rest of their days in prosperity and their years in contentment. But if they do not listen, they will perish by the sword and die without knowledge.

Isaiah 1:20
...but if you resist and rebel, you will be devoured by the sword. For the mouth of the Lord has spoken.

In the New Testament in John 14:15 we find,

If you love me, you will obey what I command.

Also I John 5:3,

This is love for God: to obey His commands and His commands are not burdensome.

Lord, help me to see that You restrain me to protect me, sometimes from myself, and sometimes from evil forces at work all around me. I know that I am often willful and not easily reined in; Your patient love amazes me. Thank You that when I have exhausted myself with my struggling, Your abundant rest is waiting for me, all I have to do is let You lead me.

"Paws"
for
Reflection

Lesson Eleven

The Master Has A Reward Awaiting You

One of the first and most important lessons we learned during our training sessions was the importance of a reward upon the completion of some act of obedience; in order to reinforce the good behavior and encourage future obedience. We learned that the rewards needed to be given quickly and generously.

Now for Cosmo a reward doesn't have to be big or expensive to be very exciting. A small piece of cheese, a bite of hot dog, or even a pat on the head and the words "Good Boy" bring a quiver of excitement and a great measure of tail wagging!

By contrast, our Master also has a reward for us, but it will not be some tidbit of food or even just a few words of sincere praise. We are told that our reward will be beyond all our limited reality now, and even our wildest imagination can conceive.

In scripture we find the following truths:

Psalm 31:19
How great is Thy goodness which Thou hast stored up for those who fear Thee, which Thou hast wrought for those who take refuge in Thee before the sons of men!

I Corinthians 2:9 says,

However it is written: "No eye has seen, no ear has heard, no mind has conceived what God has prepared for those who love Him."

Revelation 22:12 assures us,

Behold, I am coming soon! My reward is with me, and I will give to everyone according to what he has done.

Lord, it seems so often that the things we do here go largely unnoticed and unrewarded. Life is so busy, and everyone is running in all different directions. Sometimes the good things we do just seem not to matter. Thank You that nothing escapes Your complete and utter knowledge of me. You do see, and You will reward me. Help the anticipation of that reward, which will be beyond anything I can imagine, keep me going. Let my goal be to hear you say, "Well done, My good and faithful servant." Those words, on that day, will be worth it all; and the struggles and disappointments of this life will fade away forever.

"Paws" *for* *Reflection*

Lesson Twelve

We Are Easily Distracted

I don't know how things work at your house, but at our house mornings are really crazy! I am usually trying to get everything done and get out the door. We have divided the morning responsibilities for Cosmo, so on Monday, Wednesday, and Friday it's my job to get up by 7:15, feed him, and take him for his walk. I have to be out the door by 8:45 several mornings a week, so you can see that I'm dealing with a very narrow time frame; plus I have to eat and get ready myself.

This walk of ours starts out pretty well on task; focused on where we are going. That is, until Cosmo hears the first bird chirp, or sees another dog, or until the first car passes us. Instantly his attention is transferred from what we were doing, and where we were going, to this new interest. First he hears and sees it, and then he wants to leave the path and go after it.

Now because I have a plan for the day, I can't just be carried off on some tangent by this little critter, so by some means, I have to get his focus back on where we need to be; back on course. I have to admit, some days this is easier than others. It really all depends on how the distraction rates on Cosmo's interest scale. Sometimes, especially if it is another dog that has his attention, I just have to pick him up and carry him home.

Isn't that the way it is with us? We're going along pretty well in our spiritual walk, then something catches our eye or our ear, or our time and attention and we lose our focus. We go off on some tangent completely disregarding our Master's plan for us. The distraction doesn't always have to be something evil or bad; none of the things Cosmo was going after were bad, they just took him off course for my plan for him.

We have to endeavor every day to stay implicitly on track with our Master's plan for us. We have to shut out, with His help, all the distractions that call out to us.

Luke 10: 38-42

As Jesus and His disciples were on their way, he came to a village where a woman named Martha opened her home to Him.

She had a sister called Mary, who sat at the Lord's feet listening to what He said. But Martha was distracted by all the preparations that had to be made. She came to Him and asked, "Lord, don't you care that my sister has left me to do all the work myself? Tell her to help me!"

"Martha, Martha," the Lord answered, "You are worried and upset about many things, but only one thing is needed. Mary has chosen what is better, and it will not be taken away from her."

Lord, I know I am so easily distracted from following You. I don't know why I allow things to slip in and capture my attention and interest away from You. You would think that the love and grace You have shown me would compel me to never let my gaze leave Your face, but in my weakness, sometimes I stray. I am so glad to know that when I do get distracted, You never take Your eyes off me and You gently draw me back to Your path.

"Paws"
for
Reflection

Lesson Thirteen

You Aren't Always Getting Away With Something When You Think You Are

We have used a variety of leashes since we have had Cosmo. We started out with a basic woven leash, but Cosmo's sharp little dachshund teeth made short order of several of those. Next, we moved on to a chain leash with a vinyl handle. This worked pretty well until he chewed the handle in two! A couple of weeks ago, a friend of ours gave us one of those really nice retractable leashes. You can reel it out about 20 feet, so Cosmo gets a lot more exercise even on a short distance walk.

It is funny to watch his reaction when I let the leash out to its full length and give him free reign to go on ahead of me. He looks back over his shoulder at me and then runs even faster. He thinks he's getting away to run wild and free. He doesn't realize that I have just let the leash out to its full extent to allow him the feeling of freedom, while still keeping him safe in my reach.

This reminded me of when my sons were small and they would want to play "hide and seek'. When it was their turn to hide, they would sit in the middle of the den floor, in plain view, and close their eyes! They thought that because they couldn't see me, then I couldn't see them either. That sounds really familiar, doesn't it? How often do we think we can run away from our Master or hide ourselves or our actions from Him?

We think just because we aren't looking at Him, that He can't see us. Believe me, He sees, just as I saw my sons "hiding" from me; and just like Cosmo's running away was just his imagination and not reality.

My heart was moved with love and amusement at these unsuccessful efforts at running and hiding as I am sure our Master's heart is also moved at our feeble attempts to do the same.

Genesis 3: 8-10
Then the man and his wife heard the sound of the Lord God as He was walking in the garden in the cool of the day, and they hid from the Lord God among the trees of the garden. But the Lord God called to the man, "where are you?" He answered, "I heard You in the garden and I was afraid because I was naked and I hid."

Luke 8:17
For there is nothing hidden that will not be disclosed, and nothing concealed that will not be known or brought out into the open.

Psalm 69:5
You know my folly, O God; my guilt is not hidden from You.

Ecclesiastes 12:14
For God will bring every deed into judgment including every hidden thing whether it is good or evil.

Lord, sometimes I just don't understand myself. First, why would I ever want to run or hide from you, and second, how would I ever convince myself that it would be possible anyway? Could I, a mere human, ever hide myself from Your all-seeing, all-knowing presence? I must seem like a little child playing a game to you. After all, Your Word has already told me that there is no place I can go to escape Your presence. Please help my focus to be so fixed on You that nothing can distract me or draw me away.

"Paws"
for
Reflection

Lesson Fourteen

Don't Run For Every Open Door

We have to be very careful at our house about open doors. As soon as Cosmo sees daylight, he makes a run for it; and since he still hasn't mastered the art of coming when called, this could be a real problem if he got outside.

I can't read Cosmo's mind, but outside that open door he probably sees the following things: freedom, the opportunity to explore, and a change of scenery or routine.

But what he doesn't see are the possible dangers of the open door: cars, other animals, cruel people, and being lost away from the love he receives on this side of the door.

Of course, when we open the door purposely and accompany him through it, he can go through with a joyous abandon and face the adventures waiting through the door the master has opened.

Everyday we are afforded the opportunities of many new and potentially exciting doors; and there is nothing wrong with that. We just have to be sure the doors we go through are ones that have been placed in front of us and opened specifically for us by our Master; not doors opened by someone else, or doors that we want to go through just because life is hard right now on this side of the door. Many times life just seems so routine and we want a change. We often try to pry open doors that are not even cracked open a bit.

In our spiritual walk we will encounter many doors; some better left shut altogether; and some placed in front of us and opened by the Master. As we go through these, we may enter freely to find all the joys and maybe even challenges that await us. We can be secure in the knowledge that we will be accompanied by the Master; and His plan for us is always good. The hard part is waiting, listening for His voice, and not moving until He opens the door; no matter how enticing that little sliver of daylight may look at the moment. When the Master opens His door, it will be the best one for you and one that no one can shut.

Revelation 3:8
I know your deeds. See I have placed before you an open door that no one can shut. I know that you have little strength, yet you have kept my word and have not denied my name.

Matthew 7:7-8
Ask and it will be given to you; seek and you will find; knock and the door will be opened to you. For everyone who asks receives; he who seeks finds; and to him who knocks, the door will be opened.

Isaiah 22:22
I will place on his shoulder the key to the house of David; what he opens no one can shut, and what he shuts no one can open.

Lord, help me remember that not every open door has been placed in front of me by you; and although the doorway may seem to lead to an easier, more convenient path, that may not be Your best plan for me. Help me see the possible dangers outside any door You don't open for me. Help me to take time to listen to You, search Your Word, and let You show me which doors I should go through, and which ones I should just leave closed.

"Paws"
for
Reflection

Lesson Fifteen

"Come" Is The Most Important Command The Master Gives

Our trainer told us that of all the commands we needed to teach Cosmo, "Come" is one of, if not the, most important one. She said responding to this command could literally save his life, especially given his penchant for running out the door every time the opportunity presents itself. It would be a wonderful feeling to know that if Cosmo was headed for danger we could simply call his name and say, "come", and he would do an about face, abandon his course of action, and return to safety.

This reminds me of how often we neglect the "come" command of our Master. First, we need to respond to His call to us to come to Him for the redemption He bought and paid for with His own blood; then daily to hear the call to come to Him for instruction, deliverance, and peace. He waits for us to come. He is ready and able to take all our cares and burdens and truly give us rest. Can you imagine the sadness He must feel when we refuse to come and continue to carry our heavy loads?

This all important command for us to come to Him can save our lives spiritually, physically, and eternally. Knowing the depth of love our Master showed when He gave His only Son for us, what could possibly keep us from coming quickly to His loving arms?

Matthew 11: 28-30
Come to me all you who are weary and burdened and I will give you rest. Take my yoke upon you and learn from me, for I am gentle and humble in heart, and you will find rest for your souls; for My yoke is easy and My burden is light.

Psalm 66:5
Come and see what God has done; how awesome His works in man's behalf!

Isaiah 1:18
"Come now, let us reason together," says the LORD. "Though your sins are like scarlet, they shall be as white as snow; though they are red as crimson, they shall be like wool."

Matthew 4:19
"Come, follow me," Jesus said, "and I will make you fishers of men."

    Lord, how often I foolishly ignore Your command to come to you; how often I think I can manage my own life and juggle all my cares on my own. I know it must pain You to see me struggling beneath my load, when all I have to do is come to You and lay it down. You have given me Your own Word as a promise that You will take it, and exchange my heavy load for Your lighter one. Help me not to let pride or stiffness keep me bent low, but to come to You; moment by moment let me experience Your peace and rest.

"Paws"
for
Reflection

_____

_____

_____

_____

_____

_____

_____

Lesson Sixteen

Sometimes You Just Have
To Walk Through The Heat

Recently on one of the first eighty-degree days of the season, Cosmo and I were taking an afternoon walk. He trotted right along for a while, anxious to explore a different route than we usually took.

However, before very long, his pace slowed and his little pink tongue began to pant. We were only about half way home, and I wasn't looking forward to carrying a dozen or so extra dog pounds in that heat. I kept encouraging him to "come on". Cosmo began to walk and I thought we were in the home stretch, when suddenly he spotted a cool, shady spot beneath a large tree. He headed straight for the shade and proceeded to stretch that long body out full length in the cool, green grass.

He was the picture of contentment until I broke the news to him that we had a schedule to keep and now was not the time for a nap. I got him up and walking again only to see this pattern repeated each time we came to a spot of shade. After a series of these starts and stops, I finally just picked him up and carried him home! He was certainly glad to see his water bowl and get a long, cool drink.

You know, come to think of it, that shade didn't look half bad; it would have been a nice place to stop and rest. The only problem is, if I had stopped and stayed there, I never would have reached my destination.

This life is a journey from one place to the next and it is a journey with a purpose. Sure, we need times of shade and rest and God provides these for us. But there are times when we have to face the heat of the day and the battle and just stick it out. We can know that just around the corner, the Master will carry us home where we will be refreshed and renewed.

You see, that day with Cosmo, I knew some things he didn't know.

First, I wasn't going to let him be harmed or damaged by the heat, and I knew we had to keep moving to get where we were going; unfortunately, that way was through the heat.

In the same way, as our Master leads us through the deserts of our life, He will be our shield. He will never allow the heat to harm or consume us, but He will guide us safely through the heat to the next place of refreshment.

Psalm 23:1-3a
The Lord is my shepherd, I shall not be in want. He makes me lie down in green pastures, he leads me beside quiet waters; He restores my soul...

Deuteronomy 1:30
The Lord your God who is going before you, will fight for you as He did for you in the desert. There you saw how the Lord your God carried you, as a father carries his son, all the way you went until you reached this place.

Isaiah 4:6
It will be a shelter and shade from the heat of the day, and a refuge and hiding place from the storm and rain.

Psalm 121:5-6
The LORD watches over you — the LORD is your shade at your right hand; the sun will not harm you by day, nor the moon by night.

Lord, when You lead me through a desert way, help me remember that Your ways and Your thoughts are so much higher than mine. You have a purpose and plan for each step You have me take, even though I may find the path sometimes hot and uncomfortable. Help me remember there are reasons why I had to go through the heat which I may never know; others may become clearer with time. I do know that no matter how hot this walk of life may be at times, You are my shield and fortress. You use the heat in my life like a refiner uses fire to purify precious metals. You will not allow me to be consumed by it, and when the refining work is done, You will lead me to a cool resting place. Help me to be patient and trust You until I am again refreshed and rested.

"Paws"
for
Reflection

Lesson Seventeen

The Master Chooses the Direction

Each time we come to a crossroad on our walk, I know a battle of the wills is about to ensue. Cosmo has a definite opinion about which way he wants to go, and he pulls in that direction; now, this may or may not coincide with what I have planned.

You see, his choice is based on what he has to work with through his finite abilities. He doesn't have the higher intelligence or thought processes, or the concept of time and schedules, which guides me in the decision-making process.

He has no understanding of his circumstances and how past, present, and future are all connected. He can only deal with the here and now.

It's the same way with us when it comes to decisions and choices for our lives. We also are dealing with information from a limited point of reference; a handicap, so to speak.

We can see where we are currently, and we can look back to where we started, but we do not have the advantage of looking ahead through time into the future to see where we will go.

Fortunately, our Master has no such limitations. The future is as clear to Him as the past and present; time and eternity are at His command. He can move people and circumstances to bring about our ultimate good.

How foolish we would be to insist on going our own way when we can let Him choose our direction; knowing it will be the right way, the way of peace, contentment, and blessing.

Proverbs 16:9
In his heart a man plans his course, but the Lord determines his steps.

John 10:27
My sheep listen to my voice. I know them and they follow me.

Lord, I am sorry when I foolishly think I am wise enough to choose my own direction. I know that Your knowledge of my past, present, and future has no limitations. Please turn my heart to follow closely after You; then I can be sure the direction I take will be the right one that will lead me to peace, blessing, and success.

"Paws"
for
Reflection

Lesson Eighteen

Do Not Be Spiteful
or Seek Revenge

If you do any reading about dachshunds, you will find that one of their negative characteristics is that they by nature have the capacity to be very spiteful with their master or his belongings. Since they are such people-loving little animals, this usually occurs when they are left alone, and they are not happy about it. This feeling of unhappiness at being left behind can be accompanied by extremely destructive behavior.

Many a dachshund owner has returned home to find things in shambles. We got a taste of this behavior first-hand soon after Cosmo came to live with us.

We have a very busy, sometimes chaotic schedule, so we are in and out of the house a lot. We wanted to give Cosmo as much opportunity for movement as possible, so in the beginning we didn't put him in his crate when we would leave the house. That is, until the fateful day we returned to find a huge, diagonal gash in the back of our love seat. It left a gaping hole; with some fabric missing, so repair was out of the question. It was ruined.

You know, we humans have this same negative potential to cause harm because of our feelings of spite or revenge. Sadly, our likely targets are not made of fabric and foam. When we give in to these feelings, other people are the ones who get hurt. Many times, just like our love seat, the damage can be difficult or impossible to repair.

We have to carefully guard our thoughts, words, and actions. We have to remember that there is only One capable of passing judgement and exacting revenge, based on the fact that He alone is above reproach and perfect. He tells us He will judge those who persecute, spitefully use, and abuse us. He does not fail to see all the ill treatment His children suffer, and in His own time, and in His own way, He will bring about vindication and justice for each wrong suffered.

Romans 12:19
Do not take revenge, my friends, but leave room for God's wrath, for it is written: "It is mine to avenge; I will repay," says the Lord."

Romans 12:20-21
If your enemy is hungry, feed him; if he is thirsty, give him something to drink. In doing this you will heap burning coals on his head. Do not be overcome by evil, but overcome evil with good.

Lord, I'm sorry when I allow my feelings of hurt or betrayal to develop into a deep-seated desire for revenge. Perhaps it starts as a passing thought about how badly I have been treated; and then it goes a little deeper and takes root in my heart, growing and magnifying the hurt each time I dwell on it. Before long, it will begin to come out in my words and actions, not only to the person who wronged me, but eventually contaminating all my relationships. Help me to put all wrongs suffered into Your capable hands; knowing that You will right any wrongs that need to be made right, and that only You are able to judge fairly those who have hurt me.

"Paws"
for
Reflection

_____

_____

_____

_____

_____

_____

_____

Lesson Nineteen

Too Much Freedom Can Get You In Trouble

You may remember I said earlier that we started out trying to give Cosmo a lot of freedom, freedom without limits or restrictions. That way of thinking cost us dearly, including the loss of a sofa, a love seat, numerous pillows, blankets, and other assorted personal items.

When we discussed this destructive behavior with his trainer, she reminded us of something we had known earlier with our sons; setting limits really equals love.

She suggested we begin to crate him anytime we were unable to directly supervise him. She used the example of a play pen. She asked us if we would leave a toddler running around the house unattended. Of course, the answer was no. She helped us to see that we were looking at the crate all wrong. We were seeing it as an unpleasant restriction, when it was actually a haven of safety; a quiet place where he could nap until our return, just like a playpen.

In the same way, God has placed limits on us through His Word, His Spirit, and His natural laws. These limits are also a product of His love for us. His desire is to keep us safe, free from harm and evil; the perfect picture of the loving parent. His love motivates His limits out of His deep longing to do us good.

In a very short time Cosmo adjusted to the crate. Now he goes in easily, and usually rests quietly until our return. If we can just stop fighting, and see God's commands for what they are, not some move on His part to hold us back, but a demonstration of how far He will go to protect his children, then we can begin to rest in and embrace them.

Psalm 112:1
Praise the Lord, Blessed is the man who fears the Lord, who finds great delight in His commands

I John 5:3
This is love for God: to obey His commands. And His commands are not burdensome.

Lord, my foolish heart often wants to roam freely, unrestricted by any rules or restraints. I am aware that as my Heavenly Father You know that leaving me to my own choices and giving me total freedom would only bring chaos and destruction to my life. Thank You that Your great love for me, and the limits it has set, are not swayed by my loud complaints or my quiet rebellion. Help me stop fighting and rest quietly in Your love and limits.

"Paws"
for
Reflection

Lesson Twenty

Accidents Need To Be Cleaned Up Quickly

O.K., let's face it, accidents happen. It is just part of being a pet owner. Most every pet is going to have an occasional accident. A very interesting fact about dachshunds is that they can be very difficult to house break. This has proven true in our experience with Cosmo.

During those first formative months, Cosmo was living between two different places; one home on weekends, and another during the week. This meant he had two different schedules, range of activities, and rules. It also didn't help that we knew nothing about dog habits or training procedures. So, as a result, now a full year after he came to live with us full-time, we are still dealing with these mishaps, although he is improving.

Most of the responsibility is ours when we get too busy to pay attention to his signals that he needs to go outside. Once these accidents happen, it requires specific and immediate action to prevent stains and odor. There are some great products out there to remove the problem and any after-effects of it.

Because we are imperfect people, we too sometimes have accidents; only our accidents are called sin. For some of us, these accidents are a frequent occurrence; for some they are more rare and infrequent. Regardless of how often they occur, when they do, we have to get them cleaned up quickly.

Unlike the chemical agents we have to choose from which may or may not be effective to clean up puppy messes, we have an infallible cleanser available for our sins; the blood of Jesus. There is nothing that it cannot eradicate completely; however, failure to use it will result in permanent stains.

The best news of all is that this miracle cleanser is completely free to us, but it cost our Master a great price; the life and blood of His only Son. It is applied through confession of our sin and repentance. There are no hazardous side effects, just great results. It can be used as often as needed, but hopefully, the more we realize how precious this gift from the Master is and the great physical suffering our sin demanded from Him, the less often we

73

will disobey. As we grow in maturity and realize the grief He feels each time we sin, hopefully our accidents will occur much less frequently than they used to.

I don't know about you, but I'm glad the blood of Jesus is available to everyone without regard to status or any other criteria except that we come humbly asking for forgiveness.

I John 1:9
If we confess our sins, He is faithful and just and will forgive us our sins and purify us from all unrighteousness.

I Peter 1:18-19
For you know it was not with perishable things such as silver and gold that you were redeemed from the empty way of life handed down from your forefathers, but with the precious blood of Christ, a lamb without blemish or defect.

Lord, thank You so much for making provision for my accidents, my sin, through the precious blood of Jesus. Thank You that there is nothing His blood cannot cleanse if I will confess it and repent. Help me remember that this remedy, though free to me, cost You greatly; may this knowledge go deep into my heart and motivate me toward obedience and away from sin.

"Paws"
for
Reflection

_____

_____

_____

_____

_____

_____

Lesson Twenty-One

What We Want May Not Be What Is Best For Us

I never cease to be amazed at how quick Cosmo is. I can drop something, and in a flash he has it and is gone; or maybe I left some forbidden object too close to the edge of the table and before I can get to it, he has it and the chase is on. When I say the chase is on, chase is exactly what I mean. His favorite place to go with forbidden items is the dining room. Once he gets started going around and around that table, it is almost impossible to catch him. I usually have to call for back up and the two of us go from both directions to catch him. Sometimes, it's just not worth the effort it takes and he gets to keep his catch.

But, other times, if it's something that could be harmful, we have to retrieve it regardless of the time and effort it takes.

Some of his very favorite things to take off with are: anything chocolate, and ink pens.

I have no idea why in his little canine mind these items are such treasures, but obviously, both of these are things he cannot keep. Our vet tells me that chocolate is extremely toxic to dogs; and the ink pens would certainly not be good for him at the very least, and would leave a permanent stain on our carpets. Therefore, these things, were he allowed to have them would have an adverse effect on Cosmo and those around him.

Aren't we the same way? The things we want most are often the worst things for us. Thankfully, our Master knows what is best for us and what we need. We sometimes grab our object and run as fast as we can to keep it. Sometimes it may be something we can have, but many times the Master must keep things from us that might not be best for us. He is not swayed by our whimpering or the time and effort it takes to get us to lay down what we do not need. Most often, after time has broadened our perspective, we will look back with gratitude and be grateful that God did indeed keep from us what we did not need.

Psalm 84:11
For the Lord God is a sun and a shield; the Lord bestows favor and honor, no good thing does He withhold from those whose walk is blameless.

Lord, often my unruly heart is drawn to the very things that are worst for me, things You cannot possibly allow me to have. Thank You that Your wisdom is far above my own; that You know what would bring a blessing to my life, and what would be a curse for me. Thank You that You are not moved by protests from my limited point of view. Thank You that Your love stands firm, as You keep those things from me that are not part of Your plan for my life; although it may be painful to me now, it will be for my ultimate good.

"Paws"
for
Reflection

Lesson Twenty-Two

It Pleases the Master's Heart To See My Love For Him

One of the highlights of Cosmo's day is around 4:00 in the afternoon. That's when Dennis finishes his school bus route and parks the bus on the parking lot next to our house.

When Cosmo hears the air brake, he just goes nuts! He hears it even if he is sleeping. He jumps down and runs to the front door. If the door is closed and he can't see out, he looks at me with this look that says,

"Hurry, open the door, he's here, he's here!"

I quickly get him outside on his line so he can watch Dennis cross the yard to where he is. As soon as Dennis reaches him, Cosmo flops over on his back and stretches out to have his tummy scratched! I tell you the truth, that dog actually smiles! He is so happy to see his master and get that special touch.

Let me be quick to mention that this daily show of affection is not at all one-sided. Dennis can't wait to get across that yard to where the little guy is. While he is giving the long-awaited touch Cosmo so desires, he has a look of pure joy on his face. He just basks in the love Cosmo shows for him by his excited barking, gestures of affection, and by putting himself in the position to receive the master's touch.

In the same way, God's heart is pleased as He sees our love for Him. After all, what can you give someone who has everything; and is the creator of the universe and all that is? Ultimately, there is only one gift we can give our Master; ourselves and our love. Through demonstrating our love for Him, we can bring Him great joy- what a privilege, to be able to do something that would bring joy to the great joy-giver Himself.

In order for us to do this, we have to be like Cosmo: we have to watch for opportunities to receive His love and show Him our love; we have to put ourselves in the proper position to receive His touch. We must use our voice and our gestures to show our love for Him.

Do you remember the slogan from several years ago that said, "Love is spelled t-i-m-e"? We can show Him our love as we take time to get into His presence. Although even our deepest love for Him will always be over-shadowed by His greater love for us, it is an awesome thing to know that we can bring pleasure to His heart by expressing the very things He, the creator of love put into our hearts to begin with.

Psalm 18:1
I love you, O Lord, my strength.

Mark 12:30
Love the Lord your God with all your heart, and with all your soul ,and with all your mind, and with all you strength.

Lord, what an awesome privilege to have the ability to please You by expressing my love for You; that You, the Almighty God, Creator of all that is, would not only accept the offering of my love, but take joy in it. Help me remember every day to do those things that will nurture my love for You and help it to grow deeper and stronger. Help me feel Your joy as my thoughts dwell on You and as I spend time in Your presence.

"Paws"
for
Reflection

Lesson Twenty-Three

You Can Rest Peacefully in the Storm When The Master Holds You

The other day we had one of those late spring thunderstorms; it came up without warning and passed quickly. Dennis had just gotten home and we were sitting on our covered front porch.

Dennis was holding Cosmo in his lap.

As the thunder began to boom, I looked over at Cosmo. I expected to see fear, and hear agitated barking, which was sometimes his response to thunder even when he is indoors, much less outside. Instead, I noticed that he looked around, took in all that was going on around him, and settled calmly and quietly on Dennis' lap. There was no distress or panic; he even fell asleep!

Storms will surely come in our lives. They may come up suddenly, and may or may not pass quickly. It's not even a question of if they will come, but when will they come and how severe will they be.

If we are wise, we will expect occasional storms in our life. Some time ago, my husband Dennis did a sermon on storms that come to our life, and he shared some great scriptures. I remembered a recent storm I had personally weathered and thought that I wished I had had those scriptures with me that day. I decided not to be unprepared again. I put together my "storm kit", a suggestion I heard sometime ago. It consists of some scripture verses on index cards, and some other encouraging materials. I put them in a plastic zip bag, which I keep in my purse. This way, I can pull it out and be prepared anytime the skies darken in my life and a storm threatens.

I hope, that by being prepared ahead of time for the inevitable storms that will come, I will be like Cosmo and rest peacefully in the arms of my Master; remembering that He is with me. He will hold me until the skies clear again. His presence, and His words, "Peace, be still," are all I need.

Matthew 8:24-27
Without warning, a furious storm came up on the lake, so that the waves swept over the boat. But Jesus was sleeping. The disciples went and woke Him, saying, "Lord, save us! We're going to drown!" He replied, "You of little faith, why are you so afraid?" Then he got up and rebuked the winds and the waves, and it was completely calm. The men were amazed and asked, "What kind of man is this? Even the winds and the waves obey him!"

Psalm 55:8
I would hurry to my place of shelter, far from the tempest and storm.

Proverbs 10:25
When the storm has swept by, the wicked are gone, but the righteous stand firm forever.

Lord, it is a fact that storms will come to my life. They may come suddenly without warning, or I may be able to see the darkening skies and have time to prepare. Help me remember that You are always with me, and that I will never weather any storm alone. Just as I would prepare for an actual storm by having the proper weather gear: an umbrella, a raincoat, safe shelter, help me have the spiritual gear I need for the storms of life, including Your Word hidden in my heart, ready to instruct me at a moment's notice, and Your Spirit to comfort me. Help me to rest calmly in You until the storm has passed and my skies are clear again.

"Paws"
for
Reflection

Lesson Twenty-Four

Avoid Unhealthy Situations

I may have mentioned before that dachshunds are free spirits, and sometimes corralling them into a routine is not the easiest thing to do. Recently, I felt that we had finally gotten Cosmo into a good walking routine. We walked about the same time everyday, and we had a regular route that we took. He knew exactly at what point we turned around and headed for home. He would do it without any prompting from us. It was all nice, neat, and easy: begin our walk, take care of business, turn around, and head for home.

That is, until the day a neighbor who lived along this route warned us that there was a dog across the street from him who had an untreated case of kennel cough, a respiratory infection that can be highly contagious to other dogs.

Now, at this point, we had a decision to make: we could continue on our regular course, hope we wouldn't come nose to nose with the infected dog, and just take our chances. We could reason within ourselves that; chances were slim anything would happen, after all, since we didn't see the sick dog everyday. We could always walk on the other side of the street; and hope for the best. This would be a very attractive option since it would be very difficult to get Cosmo into a new routine; or we could listen to the warning we had received out of someone's love and concern for Cosmo. We could realize there was a real and present danger that he could become infected, and immediately do an about face and take a new direction; away from the danger, discomfort, and life-threatening complications that could come from not taking the warning seriously.

Likewise, God has given us many instructions, warnings if you will, out of His love and concern for us. There are certain paths that will lead us to health and well being, spiritually speaking. There are other paths that will surely lead us to contamination and infection. These warnings come from the wisdom of others, God's written Word, or just the quiet voice of the Holy Spirit.

Danger and disease abound in the world today, at every turn.

We can only be safe if we set our hearts and minds to turn at the first sign that something could contaminate us. We have to take a totally different direction. Otherwise, we could become a carrier ourselves, and by our example, infect others.

The good news is that treatment is available if we do become spiritually sick; we just have to confess that we have taken the wrong path, ask God to forgive us, and start on a new path. Still, it would be so much better if we would just avoid getting sick altogether considering the cost, side-effects, and bad tasting medicine treatment may include; better safe than sorry.

Proverbs 23:19
Listen, my son, and be wise. Keep your heart on the right path.

I Thessalonians 5:22
Avoid every kind of evil.

Lord, help me see that everyday I have choices to make; I can seek out and follow Your path for me which will lead to wholeness and blessing, or I can choose to take the way of disobedience which will expose me to sickness and distress. Please help me avoid anything that would infect me and make me spiritually sick; even though it may not always be the easiest choice to make, help me take the safe route, the path You lead me on, the path of obedience.

"Paws"
for
Reflection

Lesson Twenty-Five

The Master Will Never
Abandon You

We have had a particularly crazy summer this year, even for us. We have had several week- long trips out of town: a personal vacation, a church mission trip, and a conference week of classes. These trips basically had to be arranged so that we were at home for a week, gone for a week, then back for a week or two, only to repeat the whole cycle again.

I know this has been very confusing and difficult for Cosmo. He seems to know a couple of days ahead of time that we are leaving again. He gets this sad look in his eyes and seems to mope around.

As silly as it may sound, I try to explain to him that we will only be gone a few days, and then we will be back; we will return, we will not leave him forever. His finite, little mind, however, cannot understand what I am saying; he has no real concept of time in the same way that we do.

When we go on these trips, Cosmo is left in the best of care. There are a couple of families in our church who really love him, and delight in caring for him; but it's still not us. We take all his little comforts of home: his water and food dishes, his chew toys, and his crate with the familiar blankets. He has everything basically that he has at home, except that it's not home, and we aren't there. One lady even lets him sleep with her so he won't cry in his crate. She said he has separation anxiety, and even though he gets great care and has a lot of fun, he still misses us and probably feels we have left him, abandoned forever.

Have you ever felt that way about your Master? I have, and I think we all do at times. Sometimes when the Master is out of our sight, maybe because we haven't kept our eyes on Him or because it isn't His time to show Himself to us in a particular manner. We begin to suffer from separation anxiety, because our finite minds cannot understand what He knows about His concept of time and when we will be reunited with Him physically or spiritually. We sometimes feel abandoned in unfamiliar surroundings, knowing deep inside that our home is in another place. We take comfort in what we can, surrounding ourselves with people and things, but it isn't enough.

We take very seriously our promise to return to Cosmo, and as soon as we can, we go pick him up and bring him home. What a joyous reunion we have! He is just beside himself with happiness; his little tail is wagging like you wouldn't believe, and we are slathered with wet puppy kisses.

During these days when we sometimes feel homesick, and long for the actual presence of our Master, remember, if we take our promise to return so seriously with all of our human failings, can you even begin to imagine how God must view His promise to us. He has said he will never leave us or forsake us here, and that one day He will return, pick us up, and take us home. Then our joy will be boundless, and there will be no more separation ever.

Deuteronomy 31:8
The Lord Himself goes before you and will be with you; He will never leave you nor forsake you. Do not be afraid; do not be discouraged.

Joshua 1:5
No one will be able to stand up against you all the days of your life. As I was with Moses, so I will be with you, I will never leave you nor forsake you.

Lord, life here is sometimes harsh and difficult, and sometimes pleasant and easy; but even on the very best day, something deep inside of me tells me this is not my home; and I long to be with You. All I see around me, and all I fill my life with falls short. Help me during these times to know deep in my heart that I will once again hear from You, and finally be in Your presence. Then, all the waiting and restlessness will fade away; in the meantime, I hold to your promise that You will never leave me nor forsake me here.

"Paws"
for
Reflection

Lesson Twenty-Six

We Must Stay Faithful to the Master

A well-known characteristic of all breeds of dogs is their faithfulness to their master. We've all heard stories of dogs whose master died, and yet the dog continued to wait in their usual place for him to return; sometimes even to the detriment of their own well-being, refusing to leave their watch even to eat or drink. Reports have been made of dogs that became separated from their master, and made journeys of unbelievable distances, through many hardships to find their way home again.

Although our Cosmo hasn't done any amazing feats like these, in his own quiet way he daily shows this trait of faithfulness. I notice it most when I'm just working around the house, and he, as usual, tries to be just as close to me as he can be. He is usually beside my feet if I am sitting down on the couch. Sometimes my daily work takes me upstairs, out of his sight. We have one of those baby gates across the bottom of the stairs to keep him, and the havoc he can wreak confined to the downstairs; this foils his plan to follow me up. More times than not, when I have finished my work and come downstairs, he is stretched out on the bottom step right beside the gate; waiting. When I go outside, he waits beside the closed door until I open it and come back in. Occasionally, I have to go out a hallway door into the garage, and sure enough, when I am ready to come back inside, he is so close to the door that I can hardly open it. He is waiting patiently at the last place he saw me.

You see, in all our lives, there are seasons where we just have to remain faithful to our Master whether we can see Him just then or not. Sometimes we just have to wait patiently at the last place we saw Him, with the last word of instruction, comfort, or promise we received until we see Him again.

Now and again, we all feel like we are waiting for Him beside a closed door. Maybe it's a promise from His word we are waiting to see fulfilled; a healing that is yet to come; or any other thing we are waiting to receive from His hand. Sometimes, we have to wait through a time of silence so we can learn to really listen and hear.

We have to remember that whatever time of darkness, silence, or uncertain waiting we are going through, will pass. The door will open, and again we will hear the voice and sense the presence of the Master.

Until that time, there will surely be many things that will try to steal our faithfulness, but we must be steadfast; waiting patiently, not letting time, distance of our own making, or any other obstacle turn us aside.

Psalm 101:6
My eyes will be on the faithful in the land that they may dwell with me; he whose walk is blameless will minister to me.

Matthew 25:21
His master replied, "Well done, good and faithful servant! You have been faithful with a few things, I will put you in charge of many things. Come and share your master's happiness."

Lord, help me to be faithful to You, even when I cannot see You, even through seasons of uncertainty and waiting. Help me to stay focused on where I last saw You; help me remain steadfast, and not be swayed by the fact that I don't see, hear, or feel You right now. Let me be faithful to the last word You gave me, until once again I hear from You, and I am in Your presence. Please help me not to allow anything to steal my faithfulness.

"Paws"
for
Reflection

Lesson Twenty-Seven

You Can Only Run For So Long

I have said before that Cosmo is very proficient at running. If they had a canine Olympics, he would win the gold medal for that event. It's hard to believe that such short, little legs can move that fast, but I tell you he can make some tracks!

Sometimes he runs just for the fun of it, playing in the yard with some neighborhood kids or another dog. The time he runs the fastest, however, is not when he is running for the pleasure of it, but when he is running from us. This usually happens when he knows he has something he is not supposed to have.

He will put his front paws on the coffee table and literally walk around it, looking for something he can grab and run with; perhaps a pen or piece of paper. As I mentioned in an earlier lesson, once he has it, off he goes into the dining room and runs in circles around the dining room table. Sometimes it's just easier to call someone to help, come at him from two directions, and end the chase more quickly.

Occasionally I have had to catch him by myself, and it is no easy task. One thing that helps in those instances was a tip his trainer shared with us; she said that we should leave his leash on him at all times, even inside the house, so if we had to catch him we could just step on the leash and gain the advantage.

Well, this probably would have worked very well had we not been dealing with such a smart dog; after we had used this little trick on him several times, he figured out what was going on. Believe it or not, he began to pick the handle of the leash up in his mouth, and take off running with it so we couldn't use the "step and stop" technique! It was the funniest thing; sometimes you would just have to stop chasing him and laugh. What's really funny now is that although we don't have to use the leash inside at all anymore, he sometimes forgets it's not there and still bends his head down to pick it up and run!

There have been a few times when I have just decided to outrun him, but only rarely have I been able to.

He runs until he is tired and probably as dizzy as I am, then he just lies down and I am able to retrieve the object he ran so hard to keep.

I don't know about you, but this hits pretty close to home for me. How often do I waste my time and energy running from the Master? How often do I continue running despite His loving attempts to stop me?

Sometimes I run because I get so caught up in the pleasure and fun I am having that I forget to listen for the Master's voice telling me it's time to stop and rest. Other times I keep running out of sheer rebellion; I have searched out a forbidden object or attitude, and I don't want to stop and give it to the Master.

I block all His attempts to stop me, going round and round in circles until at last, through His loving persistence, with my energy spent, I stop and allow Him to take it.

Job 22:21
Submit to God and be at peace with Him; in this way prosperity will come to you.

Hebrews 4:13
Nothing in all creation is hidden from God's sight everything is uncovered and laid bare before the eyes of Him to whom we must give account.

James 4:7
Submit yourselves, then, to God. Resist the devil, and he will flee from you.

Lord, I'm sorry when I run from You to keep my forbidden treasures; maybe an attitude or action You've told me I cannot continue to have. I foolishly run from You, trying to foil all Your attempts to stop me. It is only when I am tired and spent that I allow You to take it from me. Thank You that You don't stop pursuing me until finally, Your loving persistence causes me to lay it down, and I surrender to Your will.

"Paws"
for
Reflection

Lesson Twenty-Eight

Don't Let Your Guard Down

As you know by now, Cosmo is a world-class chewer; nothing within reach escapes his sharp little puppy teeth. We have had several belongings destroyed completely, or damaged because they were left in his path: an expensive wallet, books, furniture, and of course, a dogs favorite item of choice to chew, shoes.

I try to keep a close eye on everyone's belongings, moving everything up high and out of reach.

However, a few nights ago I had finally finished a very long and tiring day; I was settled on the couch for a short nap when Cosmo came and climbed up beside me and went to sleep too.

I took my shoes off and left them under the coffee table, thinking they would be safe since Cosmo was up on the couch with me.

I must have slept more soundly than I meant to, because when I woke up a while later, Cosmo was up already.

Just a few minutes later, I heard him growling like he does when he's chewing on something, and sure enough, when I went into the dining room, there was my favorite shoe, completely destroyed!

I was just sick; I wished so much that I had put my shoes over the gate before I laid down; I wished I had noticed when Cosmo got off the couch; if only I had checked on him sooner when I woke up. The fact was, at that point, none of my wishes, or should haves, made any difference; the damage was done. I had let down my guard. I knew it was Cosmo's nature to destroy what was left available to him, and I didn't take the necessary precautions.

You know, we have a spiritual enemy, Satan, who is always watching for our guard to be down, and it is his very nature to steal, kill, and destroy. We are warned that he is "like a roaring lion, seeking whom he may devour." He also seems to go after our most precious possessions: whether it is our spiritual walk, our marriage, our children, our church, or our finances. He then proceeds to chew them to shreds.

The times when we are tired and sleeping spiritually are his prime times to get the advantage over us and wreak his havoc and destruction in our lives.

There is a lot to be learned from the lesson of the lost shoe: First, I need to remember to always be vigilant about not leaving my precious things vulnerable to such a cunning enemy. I can do this by being alert and keeping all areas of my life covered by prayer. I can stay in God's Word and seek the protection that comes from keeping everything in the center of His will. I can warn others to keep their guard up also; and when I have suffered loss at his hand, I can seek comfort and receive the blessed restoration that is waiting with the Master, who tells me that although the enemy comes to steal, kill, and destroy, He comes to give me life abundant and lacking nothing.

I Peter 5:8
Be self-controlled and alert. Your enemy the devil prowls around like a roaring lion looking for someone to devour.

Colossians 4:2
Devote your selves to prayer, being watchful and thankful.

Mark 13:33a
Be on guard, be alert...

Ephesians 6:18
And pray in the Spirit on all occasions with all kinds of prayers and requests. With this in mind, be alert and always keep on praying for all the saints.

I Thessalonians 5:6
So then, let us not be like others, who are asleep, but let us be alert and self-controlled.

Lord, I am aware that I have a spiritual enemy who is bent on my destruction; but thankfully, through Your Word, I know that I am not powerless before this enemy. You instruct me in exactly what I need to do to be victorious over Satan in every situation. Help me to know Your Word, to be careful that I do not leave myself or my valuables vulnerable to him. Help me to stay spiritually awake and alert, to know that the one place the enemy cannot touch me is in the center of Your will. Help me remember that with You on my side, fighting for me, all the power of the enemy is useless.

"Paws"
for
Reflection

Lesson Twenty-Nine

To Have Friends You Must Show Yourself To Be a Friend

Cosmo really is such a sweet, friendly little dog; everybody loves him. He is well known in our neighborhood both by name, and by appearance, being referred to as "the wiener dog". Just recently, he was part of our town parade; he walked alongside our church's float wearing a doggy-sized Hawaiian shirt.

He was great all along the route; people were pointing to him, and some asked if it was o.k. to pet him. Because he is so easygoing and friendly, we can feel confident to allow neighborhood children to pet him, with supervision.

He has proven himself to be friendly and approachable. He has accomplished this by some things he has done, and also by some things he hasn't done.

Cosmo always has a warm greeting for people; jumping around excitedly with lots of tail wagging. He responds to their touch by standing still so they can pet him. He doesn't ignore them, but returns their affection in his own way; with wet, puppy kisses. He's not at all shy about initializing contact. He's not standoffish; he'll come right over to you.

You know you have been chosen as a true friend if he lies down so you can scratch his tummy! Cosmo has many friends, young and old, because he has shown himself to be friendly.

Let's look at the other side of the coin: What if Cosmo didn't respond to people as he does? What if he growled and snarled at everyone he met? Suppose he snapped and bit people?

My aunt and uncle had a little dog like that. He always had a threatening growl for everyone, and usually, he nipped me each time they came into town for a visit. I was always glad to see that dog go home, and I dreaded the next visit. I would venture to guess that that dog had no friends because of the way he conducted himself.

There is a great lesson for us here: we will only have friends if we show ourselves to be friendly. We give people signals everyday, consciously or unconsciously, about how open we are to friendship.

Do we stand still and take time to be approachable, or are we always rushing around too busy for friends? Do we return affection when it is offered, or do we turn a cold shoulder? Do we take a risk and approach someone first to make friends, or do we always stand back, expecting someone else to make the first move?

So many things go into showing ourselves to be friendly: our body language, facial expressions, and our tone of voice. Sure, making friends involves risk and sometimes stretching outside of our comfort zone, but the rewards of life-long friendships are worth it.

Our ultimate friendship goal should be to be described like Abraham from the Bible was as "the friend of God". This friendship will also only be accomplished and grow, if we practice being still enough before God to receive His touch and if we return His love and affection. We also have to practice two –way communication through listening to, and speaking with our Master.

If we do, we will come to enjoy over time the most priceless gift of any friendship; that silent, no need for words, love and connection true heart-friends experience; a friendship that will last for all eternity.

James 2:23
And the scripture was fulfilled that says, "Abraham believed God and it was credited to him as righteousness," and he was called God's friend.

John 15:13-15
Greater love has no one than this that he lay down his life for his friends. You are my friends if you do what I command. I no longer call you servants, because a servant does not know his master's business. Instead, I have called you friends, for everything that I learned from my Father I have made known to you.

Proverbs 17:17
A friend loves at all times, and a brother is born for adversity.

Lord, thank You for the gift of friends who have come into my life. Show me the way to nurture these friendships and see them grow fuller and deeper. Help me follow Your example of putting others before myself. Help me to take time to build relationships and to meet needs. Help me to be approachable and even sometimes to take the first step. Help me be a friend of the friendless just as You were. Bring those who need a friend across my path. I pray You would bring me into such an intimate, warm, and personal relationship with You that You would call me your friend.

*"Paws"
for
Reflection*

_____

_____

_____

_____

_____

_____

Lesson Thirty

A Wrong Choice Always
Has Consequences

Cosmo's bedtime routine had really been going well as of recent months. He knew he could snuggle in my lap until I was ready to go up to bed, then I would turn everything off, and get his night-night treat from the kitchen. He gets a small bite of cheese each time he goes in his crate. After he's settled, I would take a second to be sure everything was turned off, say good night to him, and go upstairs to bed myself. He would quickly go sleep and not make a sound until morning.

Recently, however, something happened to change all that; about two weeks ago, we had a terrible storm here. That night, we followed the same routine as we always did, but for some reason Cosmo woke up barking about one a.m.

One thing about Cosmo's middle-of-the-night barking is that although it happens very infrequently, when it does, he doesn't stop! He will work himself up into a frenzy, barely taking a break to catch his breath!

We had an extremely busy day the next day, and I knew we had to get up early for work and we really needed our sleep. I thought that maybe Cosmo was still upset by the earlier storm, so I decided that the only way we were going to get any rest was to take him and put him in bed with our son, Joe. Sure enough, he settled right back to sleep for the rest of the night.

A couple of nights later, the same thing happened, and again the next night; both times, I did the same thing, I took him out of the crate and up to Joe's bed; knowing full well it wasn't a good idea, or really any kind of a solution at all.

The next morning, feeling extremely guilty about my bad choices of the last few nights, I decided to call our trainer, Beth, confess what I had done, and get her advice. She very nicely agreed with me that I had indeed made flawed choices; and that because of those choices, there was going to have to be a price paid to get things back on track at bedtime.

113

She gave me a couple of options, and we agreed that probably the best one was going to be to just let him bark it out. Her instructions were that no matter how long or loud he barked, the next time he starts, just let him bark it out. She said that it might even take up to two weeks to break the habit!

Believe me, at that point, I was truly sorry for what I had done. I knew that those few hours of peaceful sleep were not at all worth the high price I would be paying for them. Even worse, everyone else in the house would have to pay right along with me for my wrong choice. It was bad enough the first night when I did it without really thinking about the consequences, but I didn't have a plea for the next two nights when I knew what I was doing was wrong.

I learned several things from this little experience: first, bad habits are very easily and quickly formed, but they may be very difficult and painful to break; I also learned that what may start out as an innocent choice for the sake of comfort or convenience, can quickly become a willful, rebellious choice I continue to make; sadly, other people may get dragged along into the consequences of my actions with me; it takes a lot longer to break a habit than to make one; and lastly, the pleasure of the moment is not worth the price to be paid for it later.

Galatians 6:7-9
Do not be deceived: God cannot be mocked. A man reaps what he sows. The one who sows to please his sinful nature, from that nature will reap destruction; the one who sows to please the Spirit, from the Spirit will reap eternal life. Let us not become weary in doing good, for at the proper time we will reap a harvest if we do not give up.

Lord, I'm sorry when I let some storm in my life get me off course. Sometimes the circumstances I face seem to distract me without me even realizing it; but sometimes, sadly, I choose to do the easy thing, the comfortable thing, knowing it's not best for me in the long run. I'm truly sorry when others have gotten dragged along into my bad choices, and have also had to pay a price. Please give me the strength to make the best choices regardless of the convenience of the moment. Help me to take the steps necessary to correct past behavior and its consequences as best I can, knowing that You are a redeemer and a restorer. You are simply waiting for me to bring You the mess I've made, and to trust You to get me back on track.

"Paws"
for
Reflection

Lesson Thirty-One

Obedience Allows Us To Grow And Change

I am amazed as I look back at the things I have written about Cosmo over the last several months. I can't believe how he has changed and grown. As he begins to mature, he is becoming a lot more laid back.

Instead of running around at a frenetic pace all day, he spends much of the day resting quietly or even napping. When he does run and play, however, he gives it his all. Whatever bone he is chewing that day, he chews it with a passion.

I've also noticed that he is calmer in his approach to meeting and greeting people. He may still get a little excited when someone first comes into the house, but he soon settles back to his own business at hand, usually a bone we have given him to chew.

He doesn't run after all the things he used to go after so readily. We can usually get in or out of the door without him trying to escape. I think he has learned that where he already is, is where he needs to be, with us. I think he feels the love and affection, and because of that, the things outside don't have the same pull they once had when he was more immature.

He obeys more quickly now than he used to, and he takes correction more easily. I see this willful little creature coming more in line with his master's plan.

I see in this a beautiful picture of what I want my life to be like. I hope that as I mature in my faith and in my walk with the Master, that these same things can be said of me: I hope I can slow my pace and spend time just resting in the Master's presence, listening for His voice; I hope I will become more mellowed in some of my reactions, not jumping so quickly to my own conclusions, or perhaps at other people I disagree with; I hope that I will take His correction more easily, and need it less frequently; I hope I will be busy about the work He has given me to do.

I am very thankful that even in the midst of these changes and growth, the new calmness and peace that will come to my life do not have to mean that I will become dispassionate or without purpose; but more daily move toward the purpose the Master has for me, the very reason He created me.

Most of all I pray that as I realize more each day that with the Master, in the center of His plan for me is where I need to be, that I will settle down into His love and that all of the other things that seemed so important will lose their pull, and I will rest in Him.

Psalm 62:1
My soul finds rest in God alone; my salvation comes from Him.

Matthew 11:28-29
Come to me, all you who are weary and burdened, and I will give you rest. Take my yoke upon you and learn from me, for I am gentle and humble in heart, and you will find rest for your souls.

Psalm 62:5 NIV
Find rest, O my soul, in God alone; my hope comes from him.

Psalm 91:1-2
He who dwells in the shelter of the Most High will rest in the shadow of the Almighty. I will say of the LORD, "He is my refuge and my fortress, my God, in whom I trust."

Lord, I am so thankful that You take us exactly as You find us. We don't have to measure up in any way to earn Your love and grace, they are a free gifts to all who come to You. I am even more thankful that You don't leave us as we are, but through Your loving patience, and the process of time, You move us step by step and stage by stage to where You want us to be; a place of peace within the center of Your will, living out a passion for You, no longer running, but resting at last.

I hope that these adventures of a small dog named Cosmo have both amused you and given you pause to think.

I hope that the scriptures I have shared with you will go deep inside your heart and lead you day by day to become all God wants you to be.

Then, one day, we will hear our Master say, "Good job, well done! Here is your reward, I am pleased with you."

We will then sit forever at His feet, and bask in His love and pleasure.

*"Paws"
for
Reflection*